101 Ways to Deny Self

Timothy Williams

WINEPRESS WP PUBLISHING

Printed in the United States of America

Published by WinePress Publishing,
PO Box 428, Enumclaw, WA 98022.

ISBN 1-57921-397-9
Library of Congress Catalog Card Number: 2001091786

Dedicated to the small church of disciples whom God in His mercy brought together. For my two sons who are now my brothers in the Lord and for my wife, all of whom are gifts. Praise God for their willingness to deny self.

For what is our hope, our joy, or the crown in which we will glory in the presence of our Lord Jesus when he comes? Is it not you?
(1 Thessalonians 2:19)

Contents

Foreword

Among the more humble persons who suffered martyrdom was Rawlins White, a fisherman, of Cardiff.

He now came to a place where his poor wife and children stood weeping and making great lamentation, the sudden sight of whom so pierced his heart, that the tears trickled down his face. But soon afterwards, as though he were ashamed of this infirmity of his flesh, he began to be, as it were, angry with himself; insomuch that, striking his breast with his hand, he said, "Ah! flesh, hinderest thou me so? Well, I tell thee, do what thou canst, thou shalt not, by God's grace, have the victory."

Taken from
Foxes Book of Martyrs

Chapter 1

Prepare For Action

And apparently many who have taken pains to obtain their salvation will miss it: "Strive to enter in at the strait gate: for many, I say unto you, will seek to enter in, and shall not be able" (Luke 13:24 KJV). Christianity is a state of striving. Many will fall short of their salvation because they didn't care or take enough action.

—William Law

1

> Then he said to them all: "If anyone would come after me, he must deny himself and take up his cross daily and follow me. (Luke 9:23)

There is no option. Jesus stated in the clearest of terms, that if we want God's salvation, we must "deny" ourselves. If "anyone," Jesus said, "would come" after Him they must do three things.

1. They must deny themselves.
2. Take up a daily cross.
3. And follow Him.

This book only touches on the first requirement, the need to deny self and therefore gives an incomplete picture. This book deals only with one area of God's salvation and working Grace, the denying of self.

We must prepare ourselves to live this first requirement of Jesus. The reason for this book is to prepare our minds for action. As the Scripture below encourages us, let us be "obedient children" who have outgrown our "ignorance." In other words, let us be full of knowledge when it comes to Jesus' command to deny self. If we desire true blessings, it starts with denying self.[1]

> Therefore, prepare your minds for action; be self-controlled; set your hope fully on the grace to be given you when Jesus Christ is revealed. As obedient children, do not conform to the evil desires you had when you lived in ignorance. (1 Peter 1:13–14)

The specifics mentioned in this book are not meant as a set of rules unto salvation, but that we might grow up in our salvation.[2] A person unwilling to deny himself will refuse to pick up a cross and follow Jesus. Through their selfishness, they will forfeit the working of God's grace in their life.

While this book focuses on specific ways God will call us to deny self, Jesus does not have selected aspects in mind. Jesus bids a man to deny all of self, not preferred portions. Even the world will deny areas of their lives to achieve a goal. They might deny smoking or food in order to achieve a better life, but never become holy by such denial of self. In today's cold Christian environment everyone wants to clean up their lives, few actually want to *give up* their lives.[3] Action makes faith solid and true in our life. Without active denial of self, our faith is dead. We can claim Jesus as our personal Lord and Savior all day long, but without "action" that proclamation will not save us. People often complain about the danger of legalism, and we'll address that issue later. There is, however, just as great a danger in liberalism, of taking too much liberty with Jesus, or not making faith and action one and the same.

> In the same way, faith by itself, if it is not accompanied by action, is dead. (James 2:17)

This book is meant to encourage those who despair over the wickedness of who they are, so that they may have the fullness of the resurrected life.[4] Are you ready for the new life in Jesus? If so, prepare your mind for "action."

Chapter 2

Harsh Rules

To deny, to hate, to forsake, to lose his own life, such is the secret to the life of faith.

—Andrew Murray

2

"Who is it he is trying to teach? To whom is he explaining his message? To children weaned from their milk, to those just taken from the breast? For it is: Do and do, do and do, rule on rule, rule on rule; a little here, a little there." (Isaiah 28:9–10)

The church today makes a lot of lists. Many children remain on breast milk when it comes to matters of salvation. Babies kick and scream at solid food—any thought of discipline and denying self. Babies who need to grow up.[5] It seems everywhere we turn we see lists of ten steps to a blessed life, or four steps to salvation. Our land overflows with "do and do, rule on rule" and a "little here, a little there." Such lists never lead us to the righteousness of God. They may make us feel righteous, but it is not the righteousness of God. The true righteousness of God works in us as we do God's will hour by hour, step by step as we hear His will directly from heaven.[6] Therefore, the very last thing this book will become is a list of rules[7] for the Christian walk.

Such steps, as the following Scripture shows, have "an appearance of wisdom." We usually leave such books, magazines, sermons, and seminars with a false sense that we have gained something in the Lord. We must stop setting priorities, and start following the Holy Spirit.

> Such regulations indeed have an appearance of wisdom, with their self-imposed worship, their false humility and their harsh treatment of the body, but they lack any value in restraining sensual indulgence. (Colossians 2:23)

Rules and "regulations," when "self-imposed," "lack any value" in producing the righteousness of God in us no matter how Biblical they appear. Sadly, most churches, books, and sermons enjoy self-imposed rules, steps, and guidelines. Our sinful nature is such that we would rather have rules and guidelines that we can control than the cross of Christ crucifying us.

As Paul wrote, "harsh treatment of the body" is absolutely powerless to change us into the image of Jesus. While the world and the worldly will always think we have become too extreme in denying self, we must not impose upon ourselves rules. That will only produce "false humility" and the bitter fruit of self-righteousness. Often despair sets in when we keep failing to live up to those rules. Again, we must not impose upon ourselves a list of denials, thus usurping the Lordship of Jesus. Don't be fooled, however, the demands of the Holy Spirit and God's grace will far surpass the things written in this book.[8] At best this book is a baptism of water, an initial cleansing that prepares us for the fire of the Holy Spirit.

Strict Training

Paul taught that we all need to go into "strict training" and not be like so many believers who run "aimlessly" toward the goal. We run, but not on the narrow road. Few have a clue as to what God calls them to deny each day. We follow the will of our Bible study, not the will of the Father who is "in heaven."[9] We run, but have no goal of how to put to death our flesh. This book will help us keep from "beating the air." For like many, beating the air gives us a false sense of doing something for God. In reality, it is worse than a waste of time for we miss mercy's crown. Paul performed all this denial of self so that after he had "preached to others" he would not be "disqualified for the prize." Just because a person says, "Oh, I know I have been crucified with Christ," doesn't make it so. Paul could claim such a promise because for years he denied himself and had gone into strict training, all by faith.[10]

> Everyone who competes in the games goes into strict training. They do it to get a crown that will not last; but we do it to get a crown that will last forever. Therefore I do not run like a man running aimlessly; I do not fight like a man beating the air. No, I beat my body and make it my slave so that after I have preached to others, I myself will not be disqualified for the prize. (1 Corinthians 9:25–27)

As we just read, the grace of God will require that we "beat" our bodies and make them our "slaves." The vast majority of those who claim Jesus as Savior remain slaves to their bodies – not the master of them. Faith will require that we deny ourselves to the point we master our bodies. In fact, we will physically feel the pain as God works in us a grace that seeks to put sin to death.[11] To refuse the command to deny self is "to be disqualified for the prize" of salvation. For this reason Paul continued in the next verses to state that God was not "pleased with most of them." They had refused to simply deny themselves and have faith in God.

> For I do not want you to be ignorant of the fact, brothers, that our forefathers were all under the cloud and that they all passed through the sea. They were all baptized into Moses in the cloud and in the sea. They all ate the same spiritual food and drank the same spiritual drink; for they drank from the spiritual rock that accompanied them, and that rock was Christ. Nevertheless, God was not pleased with most of them; their bodies were scattered over the desert. Now these things occurred as examples to keep us from setting our hearts on evil things as they did. Do not be idolaters, as some of them were; as it is written: "The people sat down to eat and drink and got up to indulge in pagan revelry." We should not commit sexual immorality, as some of them did—and in one day twenty-three thousand of them died. We should not test the Lord, as some of them did—and were killed by snakes. And do not grumble, as some of them did—and were killed by the destroying angel. These things happened to them as examples and were written down as warnings for us, on whom the fulfillment of the ages has come. (1 Corinthians 10:1–11)

CHAPTER 3

Legalism and Salvation by Works

God wants to bring you into union with Himself, but unless you are willing to give up your right to yourself, He cannot.

—Oswald Chambers

3

> What good is it, my brothers, if a man claims to have faith but has no deeds? Can such faith save him? (James 2:14)

"Can such a faith save him?" A faith without works or deeds? The answer is a resounding, "No." Obedience to Scripture does not mean that a person tries to earn salvation. On the other hand, Scripture declares that without obedience no man can be saved.[12] Indeed, Hebrews warns us that Jesus is a "source of eternal salvation" only for those who "obey him" as they hear His voice day by day.

> . . . and, once made perfect, he became the source of eternal salvation for all who obey him. (Hebrews 5:9)

Obedience is not the issue, rather, *how* we obey determines whether someone is trying to earn salvation or not. Today we hear all kinds of whining and accusations when it comes to matters of obedience and works. Either people cry, "You are making this salvation by works," "You are a cult," or "I don't want to fall into legalism." In short, we can see what legalism is from the points below.

- The Holy Spirit inspiring obedience leads to life.[13]
- Holy Spirit without obedience leads to rebellion.[14]
- Obedience without the Holy Spirit leads to legalism.[15]

To simply obey Scripture is not legalism. If that were the case then Jesus, in saying we must deny ourselves, would have been advocating for us to sin.

Everyone obeys something. Even those who say we cannot do anything to earn salvation fall into a logical trap. For if the obedience required for salvation is to do nothing, nothing then becomes the something to do in order to be saved. Doing nothing is therefore the legalistic thing to do. In fact, doing nothing has become the golden calf or idol of today's church, all in the name of the Lord.[16] What people really mean is they want to go to heaven without being born again. They do not really love Jesus and complain of salvation by works because they do not want to deny themselves. They do not have a selfless love for God. Denying self *is* a salvation issue and any man unwilling to deny himself is unworthy of heaven.[17]

Legalism occurs when we obey any Scripture apart from the power of God's grace. When we in our "human effort" apply Scripture to our lives or others, that is legalism. For example, two men may be water baptized as Scripture demands,[18] but one be in legalism and the other not. It all depends on the heart and if the presence of the Holy Spirit is there or not.[19] Paul rebuked the Galatians for starting out in the power of the Holy Spirit and ending with "human effort."

> Are you so foolish? After beginning with the Spirit, are you now trying to attain your goal by human effort? (Galatians 3:3)

This "human effort," the striving in our strength and wisdom to live the Christian life, makes one a legalist.[20] In reality, in most cases, even among those who claim to be Spirit-filled, they remain legalistic because the cross has not crucified their "human effort." When we seek to apply Scripture to our lives, that makes us legalistic.

If you take these 101 ways to deny self and strive to apply them to your life you will fall under legalism. If on the other hand you prepare your mind for action, humbly sit at the feet of Jesus, and wait for the Holy Spirit to work and will these demands in your life, you will not fall under legalism but freedom.[21]

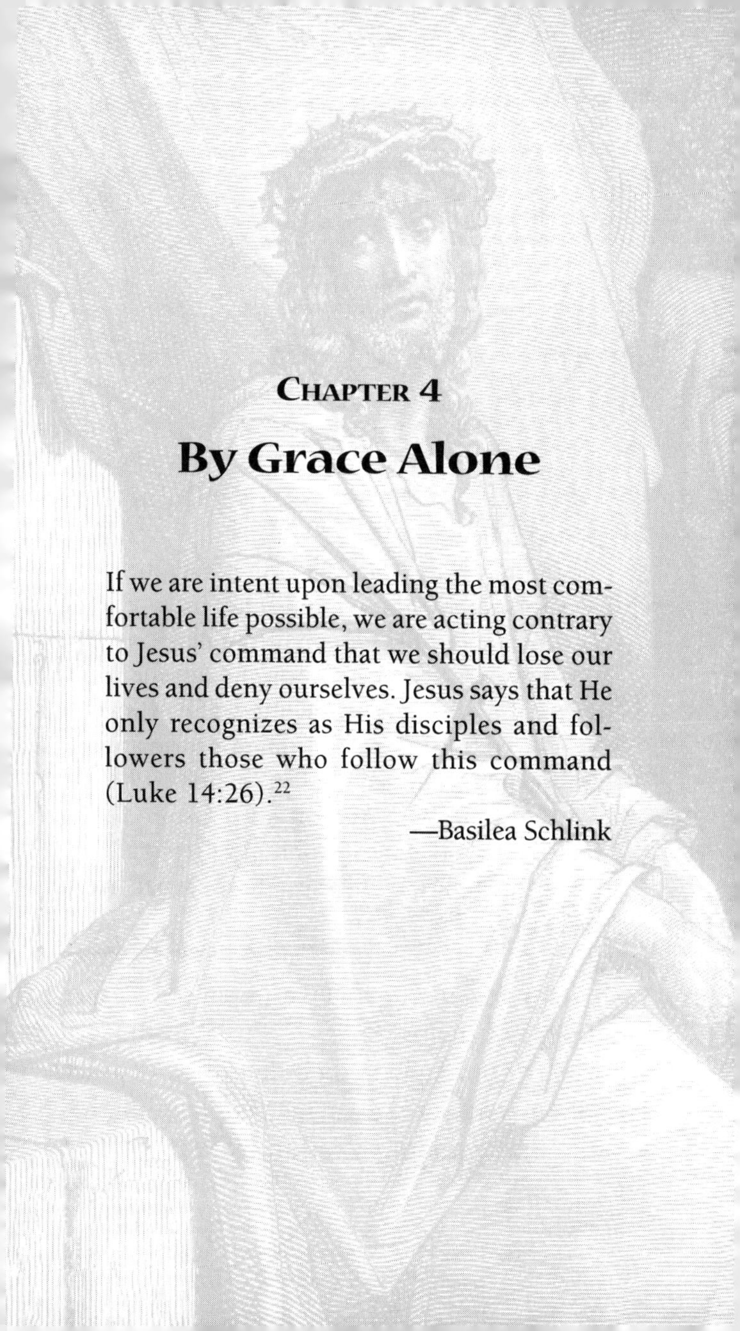

Chapter 4

By Grace Alone

If we are intent upon leading the most comfortable life possible, we are acting contrary to Jesus' command that we should lose our lives and deny ourselves. Jesus says that He only recognizes as His disciples and followers those who follow this command (Luke 14:26).[22]

—Basilea Schlink

4

> For the grace of God that brings salvation has appeared to all men. It teaches us to say "No" to ungodliness and worldly passions, and to live self-controlled, upright and godly lives in this present age, while we wait for the blessed hope—the glorious appearing of our great God and Savior, Jesus Christ, who gave himself for us to redeem us from all wickedness and to purify for himself a people that are his very own, eager to do what is good. (Titus 2:11–14)

It is absolutely true that we are saved by grace alone. The problem, however, is that for the vast majority of churchgoers their definition of grace does not match God's. So many people think that we are talking about salvation by works when discussing something to obey because they have no clue about the true grace of God. Paul wrote in Titus that the "grace of God that brings salvation has appeared to all men." And we need to get a heads up here, for God tells us what His grace truly means.

The grace of God is the power to obey. God's mercy, grace, and obedience comes from the same cloth. Therefore Satan works hard to undo the garment at the edges.[23] If Satan can separate obedience from our concept of faith, whether in doctrine or practicality, he can destroy the whole garment. And this is exactly what happens the majority of the time when someone states they have faith in Jesus to save them.

God's grace is as Titus 2:12 declared, the power to "say 'No' to ungodliness and worldly passions, and to live self-controlled, upright and godly lives in this present age." Because of this grace, Peter demanded that those who want to be saved must repent and be baptized "for the forgiveness of sin."[24] In saying this, he did not fall under a salvation by works scheme.[25] God's grace, empowered by the Holy Spirit, moved on the hearts and lives of those listening.[26] If they refused baptism, they would stop the power of God's saving grace. When a church preaches baptism, rather than the "message of the cross," legalism results.[27]

Since God's grace is the power to say "No" to sin everyday, we understand that grace is an ever-moving power. Our fellowship with God is ever growing because He is eternal. God provides more grace everyday to fellowship with Him as we grow in the Lord.[28] Just as the blood of the Lamb that saves us always moves to cleanse and empower, so does His grace. Blood that does not move dies and becomes putrid. A grace that is not always moving in our lives cannot save us if we refuse to surrender so that it might live in us.[29] Therefore, Scripture declares that salvation is an ongoing event. We were saved, are being saved, are saved, and will be saved.[30] Romans 8:24 gives us the perfect balance. We "were saved" (past tense) even though we do not "already" (future tense) have the fullness of salvation.

> For in this hope we were saved. But hope that is seen is no hope at all. Who hopes for what he already has? (Romans 8:24)

Indeed, we will experience healing all through eternity.[31] We must obey all Scripture by the power of grace. If I begin to say no to the power and demands of grace at any one point, I place myself in great danger. Since this is our time of "testing," to find out who will allow the free gift of grace into their lives every day, Jesus warned that we could "fall away."[32] This is why Paul could tell the Galatians they had "fallen from grace."[33] If they continue in that state it will be impossible for them to repent.[34]

The Galatians started out in the power of the Spirit but began to depend on "human effort" or a salvation by works. They stopped the flow of grace. And as they felt it stop, they resorted to their own efforts or someone came in preaching in such a way[35] as to remove absolute dependence on the Holy Spirit,[36] and therefore their faith died.

Gift of Repentance

As the following Scripture reveals, just as God gives forgiveness He also gives repentance. No more than a man forgiving himself or another is of any value to God, so it is with repentance.[37] We can repent all day long, but, if done by the power of self, it is worthless. Many a church and preacher demand repentance, but we fail to ask if it is a repentance of man or God?

Unless God "give[s]" it we do not honestly possess it.

> God exalted him to his own right hand as Prince and Savior that he might *give* repentance and forgiveness of sins to Israel. (Acts 5:31 emphasis added)

Paul understood this well when he instructed Timothy to pray that God would "grant" enemies of the faith the gift of "repentance."

> Those who oppose him he must gently instruct, in the hope that God will grant them repentance leading them to a knowledge of the truth, (2 Timothy 2:25)

Since repentance is as much a gift of God as forgiveness we must allow God to work it in our lives everyday. It is not as though a man can choose to accept forgiveness but reject repentance because it cost him too much. To reject repentance is to forfeit forgiveness. Therefore Hebrews 6:6 warns that if we remain stubborn against the gift of repentance for too long we cannot "be brought back to repentance." God will not give the gift again if we cross the line of trampling on the blood of Jesus.[38]

Both are gifts that a man cannot earn. It is the same as when Jesus asks, "Which is easier: to say to the paralytic, 'Your sins are forgiven,' or to say 'Get up . . . and walk'?"[39] Repentance and forgiveness are gifts we accept by faith or reject by doubt. They are gifts we surrender to or harden ourselves against. This is the decision we must make every hour of every day.

Let us put this all together by looking at the second chapter of Ephesians. For a man to cry out to God for salvation, God must give him the grace to do so. The "gift of God" is the gift of repentance worked in us.[40] We did nothing to earn that right or to make it happen.[41] Just as God created the universe out of nothing, so too in His wisdom, He created faith in us out of nothing.[42] Faith, a trust in God to do His work in us, is what saves us.[43] We trust God to work the new life in us and to save our souls. Therefore, He can continue the grace only if we remain in His "kindness."[44] As we persevere in that faith,[45] God begins to will "good works" through us that He "prepared in advance for us to do."[46] This is why faith without works cannot save a man, for such a faith is not God's faith in a man.[47] We all have need to test ourselves to see if we have human faith or Holy Spirit faith.[48]

> For it is by grace you have been saved, through faith—and this not from yourselves, it is the gift of God—not by works, so that no one can boast. For we are God's workmanship, created in Christ Jesus to do good works, which God prepared in advance for us to do. (Ephesians 2:8–10)

The free gift of grace involves three areas; mercy, obedience, and fellowship with God.[49] If I embrace the gift of mercy, but rebel against the gifts of obedience and fellowship with God I forfeit all that grace offers.[50] So let us allow the free gift of grace to flow through and, as Paul told us, be "eager to do what is good." The 101 ways listed in this book are just a few gems on the crown of grace, if we remain a people "eager to do what is good."

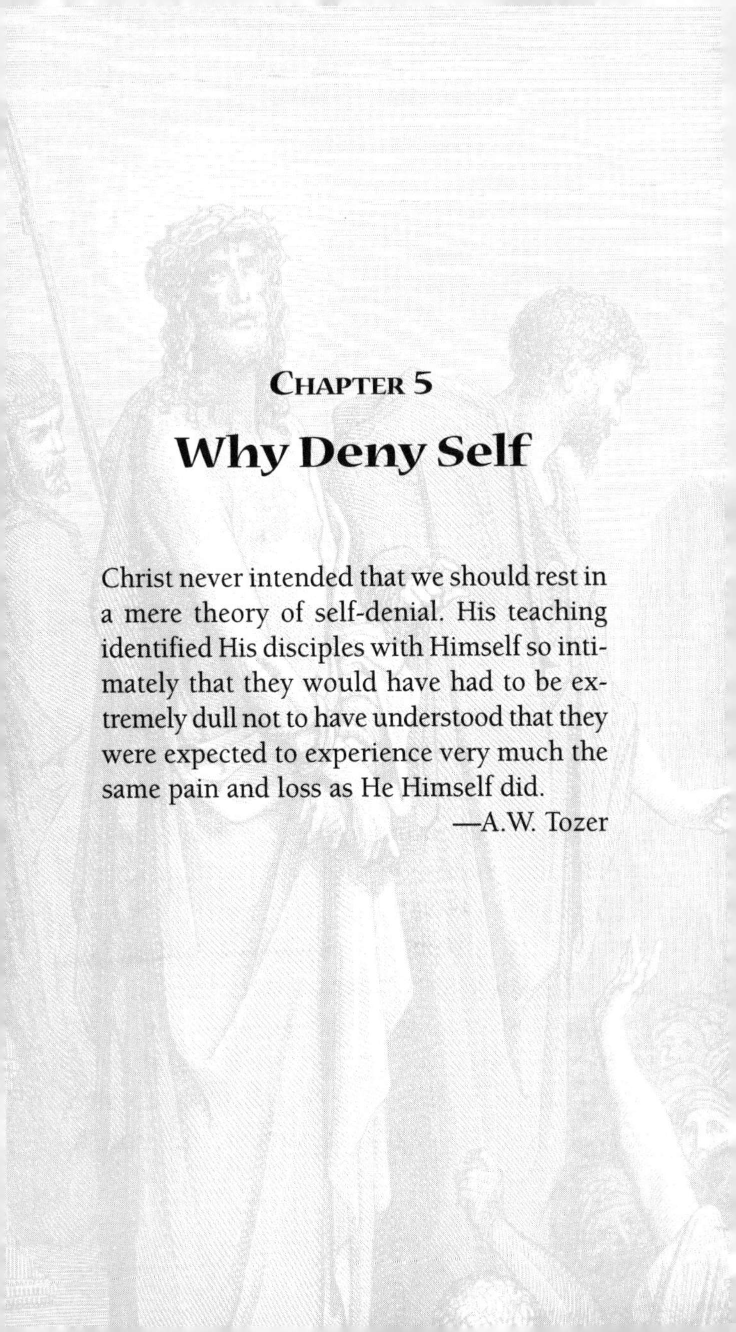

CHAPTER 5

Why Deny Self

Christ never intended that we should rest in a mere theory of self-denial. His teaching identified His disciples with Himself so intimately that they would have had to be extremely dull not to have understood that they were expected to experience very much the same pain and loss as He Himself did.

—A.W. Tozer

5

> Others were tortured and refused to be released, so that they might gain a better resurrection. (Hebrews 11:35)

Why would someone refuse to be released from torture? What did they understand about the resurrection and denial of self that we fail to grasp today? Jesus told the "crowd" and the "disciples" that everyone must deny themselves if they hope for salvation.[51] We "must," He flatly stated, deny ourselves. But why? Why does God demand such a surrender on our part?

The answer is logical and reasonable. It has to do with the nature of who we are and the condition of the world. Take for example an alcoholic. In order to be freed from his addiction, he must deny himself. There are no short cuts. If he desires freedom he must tell himself, "No" and deny himself the drink. Our self is totally corrupted. God declared there is nothing about us of any value.[52] Therefore self, all of self, must be denied, rejected, and even hated.

Jesus had to die for our sins because judgment and hell are deadly serious issues. Our basic nature causes God to wage war with us and send us to hell.[53] God is at war with the whole world and therefore we are called to deny ourselves things of the world.[54]

When a man refuses to deny himself, he denies Jesus. Right now, a very brief window of opportunity opens for people to have peace with God.[55] A peace that only happens because we let Jesus live in us. In order for Jesus to live in us, we must make room. We have to get down off our throne so that Jesus may sit down. Jesus will not live in us when wickedness resides on the throne. If we will deny our very selves, the source of wickedness, then Jesus will be Lord of our life. Anything less is a lie.

In surrendering ourselves to the Lord, evidenced by our denial of self, God gives us a cross so that we might be crucified with Christ. Since crucifixion is a slow process Jesus tells us that we must pick up this cross daily.[56] As we die daily, Jesus becomes more and more alive in us. In the end, it will be "I no longer live, but Christ lives in me."[57] But obviously for the "I" in me to "no longer live" it has to be denied and put to death on the cross. The hope of Christ in us drives those of noble heart to deny themselves.

> To them God has chosen to make known among the Gentiles the glorious riches of this mystery, which is Christ in you, the hope of glory. (Colossians 1:27)

Anyone who refuses to deny themselves only seeks Jesus for the sake of His blessings. They might use the words "deny self" and "total dependence on God," but in reality follow Jesus only for His blessings. Just like the world that uses the things of God for their own selfish pleasure, so does the Christian who denies self for the sake of self. The undenying Christian just sounds more holy than the world.[58] Self uses Jesus to gain a blessed life, which is a vile form of idolatry. Therefore, perseverance is needed when it comes to matters of the cross and denying self. God seeks to purify our hearts and motives.[59] There will be no self-centered children in heaven. Jesus tells us that only by "persevering" can "we produce a crop" of righteousness. A crop useful to God.[60]

> But the seed on good soil stands for those with a noble and good heart, who hear the word, retain it, and by persevering produce a crop. (Luke 8:15)

One of the great lies preached in the false church today is that your blessings are for now.[61] But if we do as the Scripture below tells us, and "fix our eyes on Jesus," we will discover that we must "endure" before receiving blessings.

> Let us fix our eyes on Jesus, the author and perfecter of our faith, who for the joy set before him endured the cross, scorning its shame, and sat down at the right hand of the throne of God. (Hebrews 12:2)

Like Jesus, God has set a "joy before" us and we must "endure." This is the kind of faith that the "author" of our faith began in those who come after Him by denying themselves. This faith is perfected in us as we daily deny ourselves and are transformed more and more into the image of Jesus. Are you willing to scorn the "shame" of denying self that will lead to the cross? If so you will be able to "sit down" with Jesus and fellowship with the Living God. Let us then, with joyful hearts, trust that when God requires us to deny ourselves it is best for us.

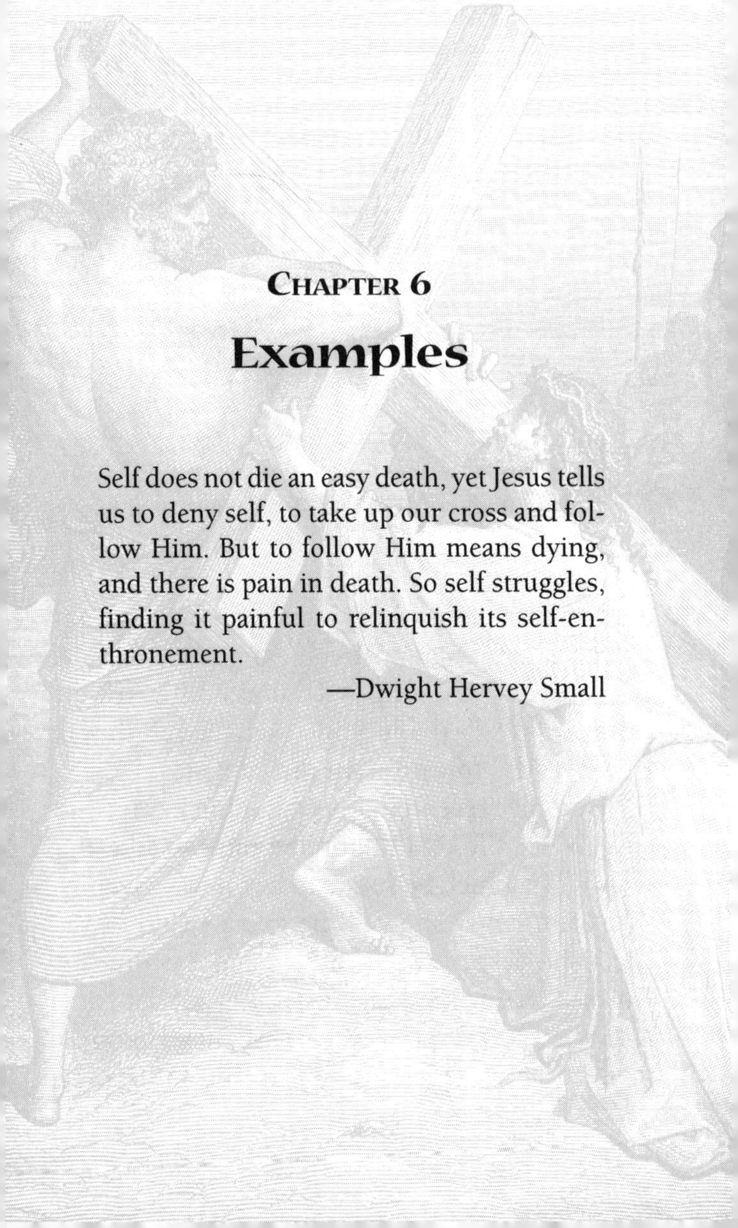

Chapter 6

Examples

Self does not die an easy death, yet Jesus tells us to deny self, to take up our cross and follow Him. But to follow Him means dying, and there is pain in death. So self struggles, finding it painful to relinquish its self-enthronement.

—Dwight Hervey Small

6

> So Herodias nursed a grudge against John and wanted to kill him. But she was not able to. (Mark 6:19)

Suppose you harbor ill feelings toward someone. It doesn't matter if you can justify the bitterness or not, you still have the sin of bitterness.[62] Perhaps you resent a rebuke as Herodias did toward John the Baptist.

Herodias resented John rebuking her for the sins in her life. No doubt she did not like the manner in which he spoke to her, always feeling that John never showed the love of God or respect she deserved.[63] So day in and day out she "nursed" a "grudge" against John. Like a baby at the breast that feeds every few hours, Herodias revisted her resentment concerning John. Like nursing a baby, it gave her a sense of self-satisfaction and enjoyment to think evil against John. In fact, she would feed this ill feeling until it became vile bitterness and resulted in murder. No wonder Jesus says the smallest of ill feelings make us liable for hell.[64] If you are angry at someone do not nurse it, deny it. Had Herodias denied herself, all her sins could have been avoided.

First Herodias had to deny her pride and openly confess this sin before God and man.[65] Then, with perseverance, she had to continue in denying self by picking up a cross that crucified the sin. Many fail at this point. They falsely believe that confession of sin is sufficient to deliver them from the sin. Many use God and His forgiveness and falsely believe that their sin is gone. If they do not see this error, they will lose the forgiveness, because while they confess sin, they remain unrepentant.[66]

Had Herodias followed Jesus day by day, denying the urges to nurse a grudge, the cross would have had time to crucify the part of her that enjoyed self-retaliation. Jesus would, in His timing and manner, cause her to dig deeper with this sin until it was put to death.[67] As she died to this sin, Jesus would have found surrender in her enough that He could fill her with His love. Then and only then she would have been an empty branch hooked into the vine. Emptied of self that would allow sap to produce fruit. All of this takes time. Crucifixion and becoming the image of Jesus is not an easy goal.[68]

Another example is the struggle with sexual immorality, a common one to all. As an older man,[69] I can tell you there is hope and victory. I too wrestled with the demands and desires of young flesh.[70] I experienced days of hard battle when it seemed victory would never come. There is no easy quick fix for this struggle, but the cross will win the war.

We again begin with the command to deny self, having a determination to deny ourselves things, situations, and patterns that cause us to sin.[71] Look to God as to how you should deny yourself in this matter, asking the Holy Spirit specifically how you must "flee."

> Flee from sexual immorality.
> (1 Corinthians 6:18)

God will show you how to deny yourself, and how to flee in your life. As you run from this sin, the hormones will still surge. Satan will advertise sexual immorality in your face and you will stumble in small ways. You must run first with the denial of self and with a cross on your back. Jesus will stand before you ordering your life as you follow Him. He will bid you to run in a specific direction. And though you may arrive at the goal line bruised, you will fall into His arms.

You will praise God for the grace that empowered you throughout the battles. I can remember when starting my first preaching job over twenty years ago, individuals told me story after story of pastors running off with someone in the church. Indeed, over the course of pastoring I watched as multitudes fell into the sin of adultery. It drove me to my knees begging for grace, His grace. I was scared to death knowing that if God did not grant the power, I would not stand.[72] This humility that God worked made me dependent on His guidance and grace. And I can tell you in weakness and humility, victory comes to those who deny themselves, and pick up a cross to follow Jesus. Though the battle is not over yet,[73] each day I can feel His power and victory gaining ground. For the yoke of righteousness is "easy" and the burden of holiness is "light." Fight the good fight, begin the battle by denying yourself and you will discover the victory that is in Jesus.

> For my yoke is easy and my burden is light. (Matthew 11:30)

Chapter 7

Denying Self 1 Through 25

You no longer "rush into the kingdom of heaven, and take it as by storm." You do not cheerfully and gladly "deny yourselves, and take up your cross daily." You cannot deny yourself the poor pleasure of a little sleep, or of a soft bed, in order to hear the word that is able to save your souls! There you are called to deny yourself, or you deny your Master."

—John Wesley

There is no middle course: we must refer everything either to God or self. If we refer it to self, we have no god other than self.

—Francois Fenelon

1

Deny self so you can have all of God.

I have been crucified with Christ:
the life I now live is not my life,
but the life which Christ lives in me; and
my present bodily life is lived
by faith in the Son of God,
who loved me and
gave himself up for me.
(Galatians 2:20 NEB)

2

Deny your good self-esteem so you can fear God.

I know that nothing good lives in me, that is, in my sinful nature. For I have the desire to do what is good, but I cannot carry it out.
(Romans 7:18)

The Lord was grieved that he had made man on the earth, and his heart was filled with pain.
(Genesis 6:6)

Surely I was sinful at birth, sinful from the time my mother conceived me.
(Psalms 51:5)

This is a faithful saying and worthy of all acceptance, that Christ Jesus came into the world to save sinners, of whom I am chief.
(1 Timothy 1:15 NKJV)

3

Deny your wisdom so you can become wise.

Trust in the Lord with all your heart, and do not rely on your own insight. (Proverbs 3:5 NRSV)

Do not be wise in your own eyes; fear the Lord and shun evil. (Proverbs 3:7)

The Jews were amazed and asked, "How did this man get such learning without having studied?" Jesus answered, "My teaching is not my own. It comes from him who sent me. If anyone chooses to do God's will, he will find out whether my teaching comes from God or whether I speak on my own. He who speaks on his own does so to gain honor for himself, but he who works for the honor of the one who sent him is a man of truth; there is nothing false about him. (John 7:15–18)

4

Deny your opinion so you can be correct in God.

A fool finds no pleasure in understanding
but delights in airing his own opinions.
(Proverbs 18:2)

5

Deny your strength so you can become strong in Him.

Indeed, in our hearts we felt the sentence of death. But this happened that we might not rely on ourselves but on God, who raises the dead.
(2 Corinthians 1:9)

And He has said to me, "My grace is sufficient for you, for power is perfected in weakness." Most gladly, therefore, I will rather boast about my weaknesses, that the power of Christ may dwell in me.
(2 Corinthians 12:9 NASB)

6

Deny your peace so you can have the peace of God.

Peace I leave with you; my peace I give you. I do not give to you as the world gives. Do not let your hearts be troubled and do not be afraid.
(John 14:27)

I believed; therefore I said,
"I am greatly afflicted."
And in my dismay I said,
"All men are liars."
(Psalms 116:10–11)

7

Deny your laziness so that you can share the good news with others.

A lazy person affects the one he works
for like vinegar on the teeth or
smoke in the eyes.
(Proverbs 10:26 NCV)

In everything I did, I showed you that by
this kind of hard work we must help the
weak, remembering the words
the Lord Jesus himself said:
'It is more blessed to give than to receive.'"
(Acts 20:35)

. . . in hard work . . .
(2 Corinthians 6:5)

Tell Archippus: "See to it that you complete
the work you have received in the Lord."
(Colossians 4:17)

8

Deny your will so you can do the will of God.

You need to persevere so that when you have done the will of God, you will receive what he has promised.
(Hebrews 10:36)

. . . so as to live for the rest of your earthly life no longer by human desires but by the will of God.
(1 Peter 4:2 NRSV)

For what the flesh desires is opposed to the Spirit, and what the Spirit desires is opposed to the flesh; for these are opposed to each other, to prevent you from doing what you want.
(Galatians 5:17 NRSV)

9

Deny your career so that you can follow Jesus.

And straightway he called them: and they left their father Zebedee in the ship with the hired servants, and went after him.
(Mark 1:20 KJV)

But run away from the evil young people like to do. Try hard to live right and to have faith, love, and peace, together with those who trust in the Lord from pure hearts.
(2 Timothy 2:22 NCV)

10

Deny your time so you can have all eternity.

Teach us to number our days aright,
that we may gain a heart of wisdom.
(Psalm 90:12)

"Be careful, or your hearts will be weighed down with dissipation, drunkenness and the anxieties of life, and that day will close on you unexpectedly like a trap."
(Luke 21:34)

11

Deny your love so you can know how to love.

Anyone who comes to me must hate his father and mother. He must hate his wife and children. He must hate his brothers and sisters. And he must hate even his own life. Unless he does, he can't be my disciple.[74]
(Luke 14:26 NIrV)

Dear friends, let us love one another, for love comes from God. Everyone who loves has been born of God and knows God.
(1 John 4:7)

And so we know and rely on the love God has for us. God is love. Whoever lives in love lives in God, and God in him.
(1 John 4:16)

Now about brotherly love we do not need to write to you, for you yourselves have been taught by God to love each other.
(1 Thessalonians 4:9)

12

Deny your husband or wife so you can become the bride of Christ.

What I mean, brothers, is that the time is short. From now on those who have wives should live as if they had none;
(1 Corinthians 7:29)

Let us rejoice and be glad and give him glory! For the wedding of the Lamb has come, and his bride has made herself ready.
(Revelation 19:7)

13

Deny pleasing your mother so you can love like Jesus.

While Jesus was still talking to
the crowd, his mother and brothers
stood outside, wanting to speak to him.
Someone told him, "Your mother and
brothers are standing outside, wanting to
speak to you." He replied to him, "Who is
my mother, and who are my brothers?"
Pointing to his disciples, he said,
"Here are my mother and my brothers.
For whoever does the will of my Father
in heaven is my brother and
sister and mother."
(Matthew 12:46-50)

14

Deny your father so you can belong to the heavenly Father.

Without delay he called them, and they left their father Zebedee in the boat with the hired men and followed him.
(Mark 1:20)

He said of his father and mother, "I have no regard for them." He did not recognize his brothers or acknowledge his own children, but he watched over your word and guarded your covenant.
(Deuteronomy 33:9)

And do not call anyone on earth 'father,'
for you have one Father,
and he is in heaven.
(Matthew 23:9)

15

Deny all so you can become a disciple of Jesus.

In the same way, any of you who does
not give up everything he has
cannot be my disciple.
(Luke 14:33)

Peter said to him,
"We have left all we had to follow you!"
(Luke 18:28)

16

Deny your guilt so God can convict you.[75]

And He said,
"Who told you that you were naked?
(Genesis 3:11a NKJV)

Against You, You only, I have sinned And done what is evil in Your sight, So that You are justified when You speak And blameless when You judge.
(Psalms 51:4 NASB)

. . . for our gospel did not come to you in word only, but also in power and in the Holy Spirit and with full conviction; just as you know what kind of men we proved to be among you for your sake.
(1 Thessalonians 1:5 NNAS)

Your wrath lies heavy upon me,
and you overwhelm me with all your waves.
(Psalms 88:7 NRSV)

17

Deny your pride so you can gain the humility of Christ.

Keep on fostering the same disposition that Christ Jesus had. Though He was existing in the nature of God, He did not think His being an equality with God a thing to be selfishly grasped, but He laid it aside as He took on the nature of a slave and became like other men. Because He was recognized as a man, in reality as well as in outward form, He finally humiliated Himself in obedience so as to die, even to die on a cross. This is why God has highly exalted Him, and given Him the name that is above every other name,
(Philippians 2:5–9 WNT)

18

Deny your power so that God can be all in all.

"I am the vine; you are the branches. If a man remains in me and I in him, he will bear much fruit; apart from me you can do nothing.
(John 15:5)

You foolish Galatians! Who has bewitched you? Before your very eyes Jesus Christ was clearly portrayed as crucified. I would like to learn just one thing from you: Did you receive the Spirit by observing the law, or by believing what you heard? Are you so foolish? After beginning with the Spirit, are you now trying to attain your goal by human effort?
(Galatians 3:1–3)

19

Deny your plans so God can have His way.

Therefore Jesus told them,
"The right time for me has not yet come;
for you any time is right.
(John 7:6)

Instead, you ought to say, "If the Lord wills, we shall live and also do this or that." But as it is, you boast in your arrogance; all such boasting is evil.
(James 4:15-16 NASB)

I know, O Lord, that a man's life is not his own; it is not for man to direct his steps.
(Jeremiah 10:23)

20

Deny self so that you become fit to pick up a cross and follow Jesus.

Then he called the crowd to him along with his disciples and said: "If anyone would come after me, he must deny himself and take up his cross and follow me.
(Mark 8:34)

21

Deny your wants so Jesus can meet His needs through you.

But if we have food and clothing,
we will be content with that.
(1 Timothy 6:8)

For we who are alive are always being given over to death for Jesus' sake, so that his life may be revealed in our mortal body.
(2 Corinthians 4:11)

. . . sorrowful, yet always rejoicing;
poor, yet making many rich;
having nothing,
and yet possessing everything.
(2 Corinthians 6:10)

I have no one else like him, who takes a genuine interest in your welfare. For everyone looks out for his own interests, not those of Jesus Christ.
(Philippians 2:20–21)

22

Deny your judgments so you can judge correctly.

By myself I can do nothing; I judge only as I hear, and my judgment is just, for I seek not to please myself but him who sent me.
(John 5:30)

But now I am writing you that you must not associate with anyone who calls himself a brother but is sexually immoral or greedy, an idolater or a slanderer, a drunkard or a swindler. With such a man do not even eat.
(1 Corinthians 5:11)

"Stop judging by mere appearances, and make a right judgment."
(John 7:24)

23

Deny your church, ministry, projects, and prayer groups so you can love only God.

He removed the high places, smashed the sacred stones and cut down the Asherah poles. He broke into pieces the bronze snake Moses had made, for up to that time the Israelites had been burning incense to it. (It was called Nehushtan.) (2 Kings 18:4)

24

Deny your Christian brother and sister so you can present them perfect.

We proclaim him, admonishing and teaching everyone with all wisdom, so that we may present everyone perfect in Christ. (Colossians 1:28)

But when Jesus turned and looked at his disciples, he rebuked Peter. "Get behind me, Satan!" he said. "You do not have in mind the things of God, but the things of men." (Mark 8:33)

25

Deny the noisiness of the day so that you can hear His voice whispering.

And these are but the outer fringe of his works; how faint the whisper we hear of him! Who then can understand the thunder of his power?"
(Job 26:14)

After the earthquake came a fire, but the Lord was not in the fire. And after the fire came a gentle whisper. When Elijah heard it, he pulled his cloak over his face and went out and stood at the mouth of the cave. Then a voice said to him, "What are you doing here, Elijah?"[76]
(1 Kings 19:12–13)

The Lord is good to those whose hope is in him, to the one who seeks him; it is good to wait quietly for the salvation of the Lord. It is good for a man to bear the yoke while he is young. Let him sit alone in silence, for the Lord has laid it on him.
(Lamentations 3:25–28)

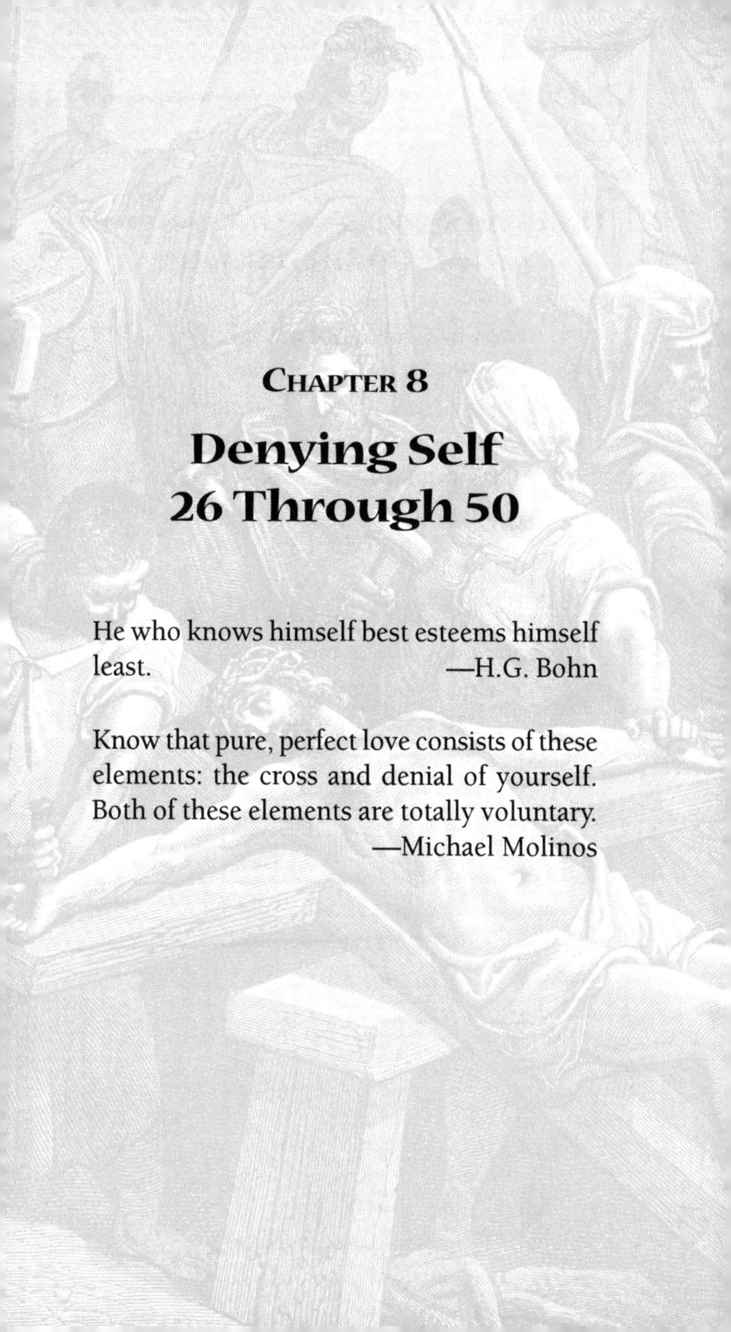

CHAPTER 8

Denying Self 26 Through 50

He who knows himself best esteems himself least.
—H.G. Bohn

Know that pure, perfect love consists of these elements: the cross and denial of yourself. Both of these elements are totally voluntary.
—Michael Molinos

26

Deny your mess so that you can reflect God's character.

For God is not a God of
disorder but of peace.
(1 Corinthians 14:33a)

The lazy man does not roast his game,
but the diligent man prizes his possessions.
(Proverbs 12:27)

When I consider your heavens, the work
of your fingers, the moon and the stars,
which you have set in place,
(Psalms 8:3)

27

Deny all of your personal items, photographs, hobbies, plans and keepsakes so that you are ready to follow God's call.

"Let him who is on the housetop not go down into the house, nor enter to take anything out of his house.
(Mark 13:15 NKJV)

"It will be just like this on the day the Son of Man is revealed. On that day no one who is on the roof of his house, with his goods inside, should go down to get them. Likewise, no one in the field should go back for anything. Remember Lot's wife!
(Luke 17:30–32)

28

Deny your education so you can have the mind of Christ.

But whatever was to my profit I now consider loss for the sake of Christ. What is more, I consider everything a loss compared to the surpassing greatness of knowing Christ Jesus my Lord, for whose sake I have lost all things. I consider them rubbish, that I may gain Christ.
(Philippians 3:7–8)

Now when they saw the boldness of Peter and John, and perceived that they were uneducated and untrained men, they marveled. And they realized that they had been with Jesus.
(Acts 4:13 NKJV)

29

Deny dating so you can live only for Jesus.

Are you unmarried?
Do not look for a wife.
(1 Corinthians 7:27)

Treat . . . older women as mothers,
and younger women as sisters,
with absolute purity.
(1 Timothy 5:2)

30

Deny your gossip so that you can celebrate the Truth.

A gossip's whispers are savoury morsels,
gulped down into the inner man.
(Proverbs 18:8 NEB)

Make it your ambition to lead a quiet life,
to mind your own business . . .
(1 Thessalonians 4:11)

31

Deny your tranquility so you can suffer with Christ.

Now if we are children, then we are heirs—heirs of God and co-heirs with Christ, if indeed we share in his sufferings in order that we may also share in his glory.
(Romans 8:17)

I am happy in my sufferings for you. There are many things that Christ must still suffer through his body, the church. I am accepting my part of these things that must be suffered. I accept these sufferings in my body. I suffer for his body, the Church.
(Colossians 1:24 EVD)

For it has been granted to you on behalf of Christ not only to believe on him, but also to suffer for him,
(Philippians 1:29)

32

Deny your possessions that your church might reflect the love of heaven.

All the believers were together and had
everything in common. Selling their
possessions and goods, they gave to
anyone as he had need.
(Acts 2:44–45)

No one claimed that any of his
possessions was his own,
but they shared everything they had.
(Acts 4:32b)

33

Deny your heart so that you, the church, can become one in heart and mind.

All the believers were one in
heart and mind.
(Acts 4:32)

I appeal to you, brothers, in the name of our Lord Jesus Christ, that all of you agree with one another so that there may be no divisions among you and that you may be perfectly united in mind and thought.
(1 Corinthians1:10)

All of us who are spiritually mature should think this way, too. And if there are things you do not agree with, God will make them clear to you.
(Philippians 3:15 NCV)

34

Deny your commentaries so you can hear the voice of Truth.[77]

But Samuel replied: "Does the Lord delight in burnt offerings and sacrifices as much as in obeying the voice of the Lord? To obey is better than sacrifice, and to heed is better than the fat of rams.
(1 Samuel 15:22)

Samuel did not yet know the Lord, and the Lord had not spoken directly to him yet. The Lord called Samuel for the third time. Samuel got up and went to Eli and said, "I am here. You called me." Then Eli realized the Lord was calling the boy.
(1 Samuel 3:7–8 NCV)

The watchman opens the gate for him, and the sheep listen to his voice. He calls his own sheep by name and leads them out. When he has brought out all his own, he goes on ahead of them, and his sheep follow him because they know his voice. But they will never follow a stranger; in fact, they will run away from him because they do not recognize a stranger's voice."
(John 10:3–5)

35

Deny your Greek and Hebrew so you can preach the living word of God.

Where is the wise man? Where is the scholar? Where is the philosopher of this age? Has not God made foolish the wisdom of the world?
(1 Corinthians 1:20)

At this I fell at his feet to worship him. But he said to me, "Do not do it! I am a fellow servant with you and with your brothers who hold to the testimony of Jesus. Worship God! For the testimony of Jesus is the spirit of prophecy."
(Revelation 19:10)

. . . Greeks look for wisdom,[78]
(1 Corinthians 1:22)

36

Deny your children so you can give them to God.

"Do not lay a hand on the boy," he said. "Do not do anything to him. Now I know that you fear God, because you have not withheld from me your son, your only son."
(Genesis 22:12)

When the time of their purification according to the Law of Moses had been completed, Joseph and Mary took him to Jerusalem to present him to the Lord (as it is written in the Law of the Lord, "Every firstborn male is to be consecrated to the Lord"),
(Luke 2:22–23)

I prayed for this child, and the Lord has granted me what I asked of him. So now I give him to the Lord. For his whole life he will be given over to the Lord." And he worshiped the Lord there.
(1 Samuel 1:27–28)

37

Deny getting meaning and purpose out of life so that Jesus can be your only satisfaction.

"Meaningless! Meaningless!" says
the Teacher. "Utterly meaningless!
Everything is meaningless."
(Ecclesiastes 1:2)

To Adam he said, "Because you listened to your wife and ate from the tree about which I commanded you, 'You must not eat of it,' "Cursed is the ground because of you; through painful toil you will eat of it all the days of your life.
(Genesis 3:17)

I devoted myself to study and to explore by wisdom all that is done under heaven. What a heavy burden God has laid on men! I have seen all the things that are done under the sun; all of them are meaningless, a chasing after the wind.
(Ecclesiastes 1:13–14)

38

Deny sports so that you will not have any high places.

. . . those who use the things of the world,
as if not engrossed in them.
For this world in its present form
is passing away.
(1 Corinthians 7:31)

. . . lovers of pleasure
rather than lovers of God
(2 Timothy 3:4)

The Israelites secretly did things against the Lord their God that were not right. From watchtower to fortified city they built themselves high places in all their towns.
(2 Kings 17:9)

39

Deny yourself vacations so you can become a prisoner of Jesus.

So do not be ashamed to testify about
our Lord, or ashamed of me his prisoner.
But *join with me* in suffering for the gospel,
by the power of God,
(2 Timothy 1:8)

But he said to them, "I have food to eat
that you know nothing about." Then his
disciples said to each other, "Could
someone have brought him food?" "My
food," said Jesus, "is to do the will of him
who sent me and to finish his work.
(John 4:32–34)

To this very hour we go
hungry and thirsty,
we are in rags,
we are brutally treated,
we are homeless.
(1 Corinthians 4:11)

40

Deny your health so you can waste away for the gospel.

Therefore we do not lose heart.
Though outwardly we are wasting away, yet inwardly we are being renewed day by day.
(2 Corinthians 4:16)

As you know, it was because of an illness that I first preached the gospel to you.
(Galatians 4:13)

41

Deny your humor so you can talk like Jesus.

Nor should there be obscenity,
foolish talk or coarse joking,
which are out of place,
but rather thanksgiving.
(Ephesians 5:4)

Is anyone happy?
Let him sing songs of praise.
(James 5:13)

42

Deny your chatter so that others will benefit from what they hear.

Do not let any unwholesome talk come out of your mouths, but only what is helpful for building others up according to their needs, that it may benefit those who listen.
(Ephesians 4:29)

But avoid worldly and empty chatter, for it will lead to further ungodliness,
(2 Timothy 2:16 NASB)

O Timothy, guard what has been entrusted to you, avoiding worldly and empty chatter and the opposing arguments of what is falsely called "knowledge"—which some have professed and thus gone astray from the faith. Grace be with you.
(1 Timothy 6:20-21 NNAS)

43

Deny what you see so you can walk by faith.

We live by faith, not by sight.
(2 Corinthians 5:7)

Now faith is being sure of what we hope for and certain of what we do not see.
(Hebrews 11:1)

But when he saw the wind, he was afraid and, beginning to sink, cried out, "Lord, save me!"
(Matthew 14:30)

So the soldiers cut the ropes that held the lifeboat and let it fall away.[79]
(Acts 27:32)

44

Deny your food budget so that you can feed thousands.

But he answered, "You give them something to eat." They said to him, "That would take eight months of a man's wages ! Are we to go and spend that much on bread and give it to them to eat?" "How many loaves do you have?" he asked. "Go and see." When they found out, they said, "Five—and two fish." Then Jesus directed them to have all the people sit down in groups on the green grass. So they sat down in groups of hundreds and fifties. Taking the five loaves and the two fish and looking up to heaven, he gave thanks and broke the loaves. Then he gave them to his disciples to set before the people. He also divided the two fish among them all. They all ate and were satisfied,

(Mark 6:37–42)

45

Deny your home so you can have a home in heaven.

"I tell you the truth," Jesus replied, "no one who has left home or brothers or sisters or mother or father or children or fields for me and the gospel will fail to receive a hundred times as much in this present age (homes, brothers, sisters, mothers, children and fields—and with them, persecutions) and in the age to come, eternal life.
(Mark 10:29–30)

. . . having nothing,
and yet possessing everything.
(2 Corinthians 6:10)

By faith he made his home in the promised land like a stranger in a foreign country; he lived in tents, as did Isaac and Jacob, who were heirs with him of the same promise.
(Hebrews 11:9)

Blessed are those whose strength is in you, who have set their hearts on pilgrimage.
(Psalms 84:5)

46

Deny your popularity so you can hear God's will.

. . . and when they found him,
they exclaimed:
"Everyone is looking for you!"
Jesus replied, "Let us go somewhere else
—to the nearby villages—
so I can preach there also.
That is why I have come."
(Mark 1:37–38)

47

Deny your pleasing of men so you can be free from the snares of men.

Fear of man will prove to be a snare, but whoever trusts in the Lord is kept safe. (Proverbs 29:25)

Am I now trying to win the approval of men, or of God? Or am I trying to please men? If I were still trying to please men, I would not be a servant of Christ. (Galatians 1:10)

They came to him and said, "Teacher, we know you are a man of integrity. You aren't swayed by men, because you pay no attention to who they are; but you teach the way of God in accordance with the truth. Is it right to pay taxes to Caesar or not? (Mark 12:14)

As for those who seemed to be important—whatever they were makes no difference to me; God does not judge by external appearance—those men added nothing to my message. (Galatians 2:6)

48

Deny your wasting of time so you can know God's will.

Be very careful, then, how you live—not as unwise but as wise, making the most of every opportunity, because the days are evil. Therefore do not be foolish, but understand what the Lord's will is. (Ephesians 5:15–17)

"The harvest is past,
the summer has ended,
and we are not saved."
(Jeremiah 8:20)

49

Deny your lusts, possessions, projects, and plans so you can love only Him.

For everything in the world—the cravings of sinful man, the lust of his eyes and the boasting of what he has and does—comes not from the Father but from the world.
(1 John 2:16)

. . . the twenty-four elders will fall down before Him who sits on the throne, and will worship Him who lives forever and ever, and will cast their crowns before the throne, . . .
(Revelation 4:10 NASB)

And they said,
"Come, let us build ourselves a city,
and a tower whose top is in the heavens;
let us make a name for ourselves, . . ."
(Genesis 11:4 NKJV)

50

Deny your sleep so that you can pray.

One of those days Jesus went out to
a mountainside to pray, and spent
the night praying to God.
(Luke 6:12)

But Jesus often withdrew to lonely
places and prayed.
(Luke 5:16)

Very early in the morning,
while it was still dark,
Jesus got up, left the house
and went off to a solitary place,
where he prayed.
(Mark 1:35)

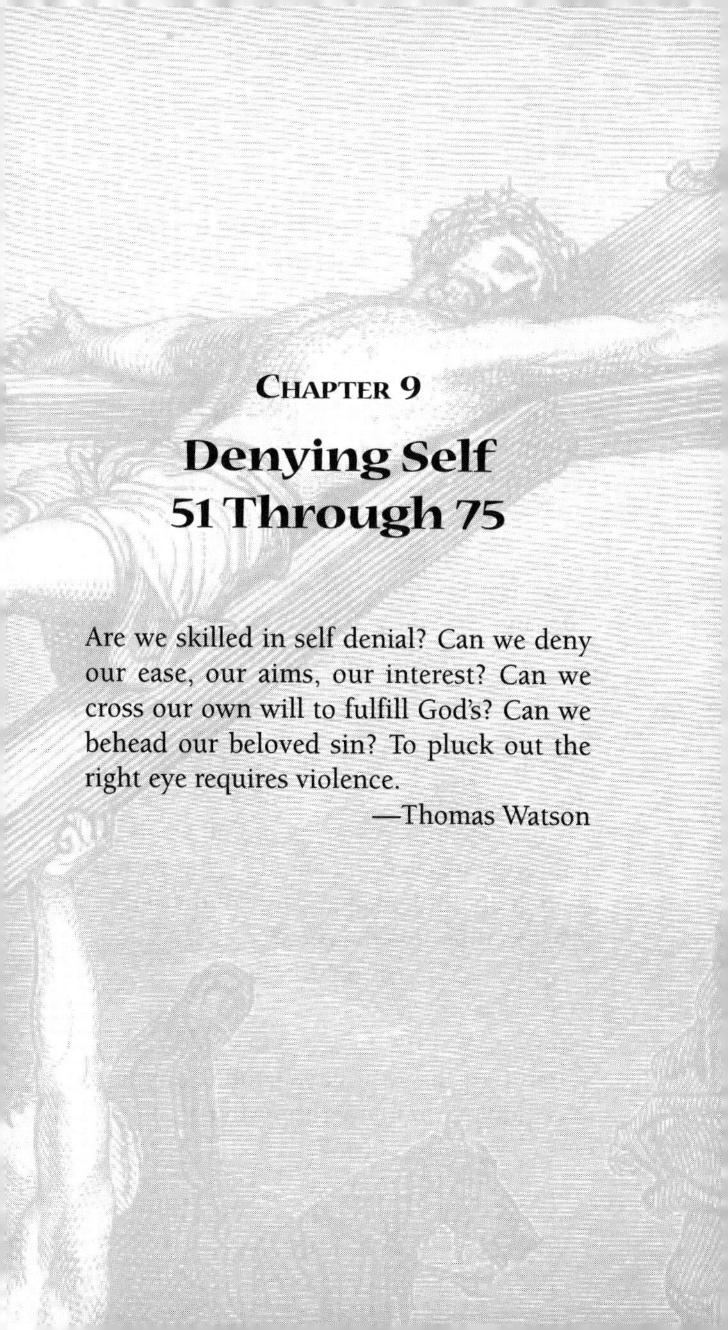

Chapter 9

Denying Self 51 Through 75

Are we skilled in self denial? Can we deny our ease, our aims, our interest? Can we cross our own will to fulfill God's? Can we behead our beloved sin? To pluck out the right eye requires violence.

—Thomas Watson

51

Deny your doctrine so you can have sound doctrine.

For the time will come when men will not put up with sound doctrine. Instead, to suit their own desires, they will gather around them a great number of teachers to say what their itching ears want to hear. (2 Timothy 4:3)

Jesus replied, "You are in error because you do not know the Scriptures or the power of God. (Matthew 22:29)

As for you, the anointing you received from him remains in you, and you do not need anyone to teach you. But as his anointing teaches you about all things and as that anointing is real, not counterfeit— just as it has taught you, remain in him. (1 John 2:27)

Thus you nullify the word of God by your tradition that you have handed down. And you do many things like that." (Mark 7:13)

52

Deny your arguments so you can become pure.

Don't have anything to do with foolish and stupid arguments, because you know they produce quarrels. And the Lord's servant must not quarrel; instead, he must be kind to everyone, able to teach, not resentful. (2 Timothy 2:23–24)

Keep reminding them of these things. Warn them before God against quarreling about words; it is of no value, and only ruins those who listen. (2 Timothy 2:14)

53

Deny your justifications so you can be justified in Christ.

"I tell you that this man, rather than the other, went home justified before God. For everyone who exalts himself will be humbled, and he who humbles himself will be exalted."
(Luke 18:14)

All have turned aside, together they have become useless; there is none who does good, there is not even one."
(Romans 3:12 NNAS)

The Lord was grieved
that he had made man on the earth,
and his heart was filled with pain.
(Genesis 6:6)

"Why do you call me good?"
Jesus answered. "No one is good—
except God alone.
(Mark 10:18)

54

Deny your sluggishness so you can awaken in Christ.

. . . for it is light that makes everything visible. This is why it is said: "Wake up, O sleeper, rise from the dead, and Christ will shine on you."
(Ephesians 5:14)

The sluggard craves and gets nothing, but the desires of the diligent are fully satisfied.
(Proverbs 13:4)

A sluggard does not plow in season; so at harvest time he looks but finds nothing.
(Proverbs 20:4)

55

Deny your food, what you like to eat, so you can eat hidden manna and sit at the table with Jesus in heaven.

Their destiny is destruction, their god is their stomach, and their glory is in their shame. Their mind is on earthly things. (Philippians 3:19)

At that time Jesus went through the grainfields on the Sabbath. His disciples were hungry and began to pick some heads of grain and eat them. (Matthew 12:1)

They ate till they had more than enough, for he had given them what they craved. But before they turned from the food they craved, even while it was still in their mouths, God's anger rose against them; he put to death the sturdiest among them, cutting down the young men of Israel. (Psalm 78:29–31)

56

Deny your religious or spiritual sounding words so you can speak the living words of God.

If anyone speaks, he should do it as one speaking the very words of God. If anyone serves, he should do it with the strength God provides, so that in all things God may be praised through Jesus Christ. To him be the glory and the power for ever and ever.
Amen.
(1 Peter 4:11)

57

Deny your racial heritage so you can become a child of God.

Here there is no Greek or Jew, circumcised or uncircumcised, barbarian, Scythian, slave or free, but Christ is all, and is in all.
(Colossians 3:11)

There is neither Jew nor Greek, slave nor free, male nor female, for you are all one in Christ Jesus.
(Galatians 3:28)

The Israelites journeyed from Rameses to Succoth. There were about six hundred thousand men on foot, besides women and children. Many other people went up with them, as well as large droves of livestock, both flocks and herds.
(Exodus 12:37–38)

58

Deny your stuffed belly so you can hunger for Jesus.

Woe to you who are well fed now,
for you will go hungry.
(Luke 6:25)

I have labored and toiled and have often gone without sleep; I have known hunger and thirst and have often gone without food; I have been cold and naked.
(2 Corinthians 11:27)

Blessed are those
who hunger and thirst for righteousness,
for they will be filled.
(Matthew 5:6)

59

Deny your good looks so you can look ugly with Jesus.

He grew up before him like a tender shoot, and like a root out of dry ground. He had no beauty or majesty to attract us to him, nothing in his appearance that we should desire him. He was despised and rejected by men, a man of sorrows, and familiar with suffering. Like one from whom men hide their faces he was despised, and we esteemed him not.
(Isaiah 53:2–3)

Charm is deceptive, and beauty is fleeting; but a woman who fears the Lord is to be praised.
(Proverbs 31:30)

So then, banish anxiety from your heart and cast off the troubles of your body, for youth and vigor are meaningless.
(Ecclesiastes 11:10)

60

Deny your feelings so you can love others.

Jesus wept.
(John 11:35)[80]

Rejoice with those who rejoice;
mourn with those who mourn.
(Romans 12:15)

If one member suffers,
all suffer together with it;
if one member is honored,
all rejoice together with it.
(1 Corinthians 12:26 NRSV)

61

Deny your country so you can have a heavenly home.

People who say such things show that they are looking for a country of their own. If they had been thinking of the country they had left, they would have had opportunity to return. Instead, they were longing for a better country—a heavenly one. Therefore God is not ashamed to be called their God, for he has prepared a city for them.
(Hebrews 11:14–16)

But in keeping with his promise we are looking forward to a new heaven and a new earth, the home of righteousness.
(2 Peter 3:13)

62

Deny your hope so you can have hope in heaven.

You were wearied by all your ways,
but you would not say, 'It is hopeless.'
You found renewal of your strength,
and so you did not faint.
(Isaiah 57:10)

. . . the faith and love that spring from the hope that is stored up for you in heaven and that you have already heard about in the word of truth, the gospel that has come to you. All over the world this gospel is bearing fruit and growing, just as it has been doing among you since the day you heard it and understood God's grace in all its truth.
(Colossians 1:5–6)

63

Deny long hair on men so you can be presentable to Jesus.

Does not the very nature of things
teach you that if a man has long hair,
it is a disgrace to him,
(1 Corinthians 11:14)[81]

64

Deny your stylish clothes so you can dress properly before Jesus.

I also want women to dress modestly, with decency and propriety, not with braided hair or gold or pearls or expensive clothes, (1 Timothy 2:9)

Do not wear clothes of wool and linen woven together. (Deuteronomy 22:11)

You foolish people! Did not the one who made the outside make the inside also? (Luke 11:40)

65

Deny your comfort so you can suffer in your body against sin.

Therefore, since Christ suffered in his body, arm yourselves also with the same attitude, because he who has suffered in his body is done with sin.
(1 Peter 4:1)

And I'll say to myself, "You have plenty of good things laid up for many years. Take life easy; eat, drink and be merry."' "But God said to him, 'You fool! This very night your life will be demanded from you. Then who will get what you have prepared for yourself?'
(Luke 12:19-20)

66

Deny your spiritual emotions so you can test all things.

When the woman saw
that the fruit of the tree was good for food
and pleasing to the eye,
and also desirable for gaining wisdom,
she took some and ate it.
She also gave some to her husband,
who was with her,
and he ate it.
(Genesis 3:6)

Test everything.
(1 Thessalonians 5:21)

67

Deny your blessings so you can first obey God's commands.

Let me understand the teaching of your precepts; then I will meditate on your wonders.
(Psalm 119:27)

Some time later God tested Abraham. He said to him, "Abraham!" "Here I am," he replied. Then God said, "Take your son, your only son, Isaac, whom you love, and go to the region of Moriah. Sacrifice him there as a burnt offering on one of the mountains I will tell you about."
(Genesis 22:1–2)

"Nevertheless do not rejoice in this, that the spirits are subject to you, but rather rejoice because your names are written in heaven."
(Luke 10:20 NKJV)[82]

All these people were still living by faith when they died. They did not receive the things promised; they only saw them and welcomed them from a distance. And they admitted that they were aliens and strangers on earth.
(Hebrews 11:13)

68

Deny women in leadership so that God can become head over all.

I do not permit a woman to teach
or to have authority over a man;
she must be silent.
(1 Timothy 2:12)

For God is not a God of disorder but of peace. As in all the congregations of the saints, women should remain silent in the churches. They are not allowed to speak, but must be in submission, as the Law says. If they want to inquire about something, they should ask their own husbands at home; for it is disgraceful for a woman to speak in the church.
(1 Corinthians 14:33–35)

69

Deny attention to yourself so you can only see God's goodness.

Above him were seraphs, each with six wings: *With two wings they covered their faces, with two they covered their feet*, and with two they were flying. And they were calling to one another: "Holy, holy, holy is the Lord Almighty; the whole earth is full of his glory." At the sound of their voices the doorposts and thresholds shook and the temple was filled with smoke.[83]
(Isaiah 6:2–4)

Your heart became proud on account of your beauty, and you corrupted your wisdom because of your splendor. So I threw you to the earth; I made a spectacle of you before kings.
(Ezekiel 28:17)

. . . the twenty-four elders fall down before him who sits on the throne, and worship him who lives for ever and ever. They lay their crowns before the throne and say: "You are worthy, our Lord and God, to receive glory and honor and power, for you created all things, and by your will they were created and have their being."
(Revelation 4:10–11)

70

Deny your dealing with sin so you can gain power over sin.

For if you live according to the sinful nature, you will die; but if by the Spirit you put to death the misdeeds of the body, you will live,
(Romans 8:13)

71

Deny your Bible study so you can follow Jesus.

You diligently study the Scriptures because you think that by them you possess eternal life. These are the Scriptures that testify about me, yet you refuse to come to me to have life.
(John 5:39–40)

Do your best to present yourself to God as one approved, a workman who does not need to be ashamed and who correctly handles the word of truth.[84]
(2 Timothy 2:15)

Reflect on what I am saying, for the Lord will give you insight into all this.
(2 Timothy 2:7)

Take the helmet of salvation and the *sword of the Spirit*, which is the word of God.
(Ephesians 6:17)

72

Deny your cross so you can carry His cross.

I tell you the truth, when you were younger you dressed yourself and went where you wanted; but when you are old you will stretch out your hands, and someone else will dress you and lead you where you do not want to go."
Jesus said this to indicate the kind of death by which Peter would glorify God.
Then he said to him, "Follow me!"
(John 21:18–19)

73

Deny all your quarreling with God so you can become pure in heart.

In all this,
Job did not sin by charging
God with wrongdoing.
(Job 1:22)

Blessed are the pure in heart,
for they will see God.
(Matthew 5:8)

All the words of my mouth are just;
none of them is crooked or perverse.
To the discerning all of them are right;
they are faultless to those
who have knowledge.
(Proverbs 8:8–9)

74

Deny your politics so you can govern with Jesus.[85]

No one serving as a soldier gets involved
in civilian affairs—he wants to please
his commanding officer.
(2 Timothy 2:4)

75

Deny short hair on women so they can reflect the glory God intended.

. . . but that if a woman has long hair,
it is her glory?
For long hair is given to
her as a covering.
(1 Corinthians 11:15)

Chapter 10

Denying Self 76 Through 101

Jesus also warned that only those who do the will of His Father are His brothers and sisters. Jesus often said nothing at all about faith when He called people to salvation. He told seekers to deny themselves, take up their crosses and follow Him lest they forfeit their souls. He called people to costly discipleship and sincere submission, a true faith.

—David S. Kirkwood

76

Deny your awards, trophies, and certificates so you can receive a crown of life.

But all such assets I have written off because of Christ. I would say more: I count everything sheer loss, because all is far outweighed by the gain of knowing Christ Jesus my Lord, for whose sake I did in fact lose everything. I count it so much garbage, for the sake of gaining Christ (Philippians 3:7 NEB)

For all that is in the world,
the lust of the flesh
and the lust of the eyes
and the boastful pride of life,
is not from the Father,
but is from the world.
(1 John 2:16 NNAS)

77

Deny your psychologist, "Christian" counselor, and self-help books so you can become sane in Jesus.

See to it that no one takes you captive through hollow and deceptive philosophy, which depends on human tradition and the basic principles of this world rather than on Christ.
(Colossians 2:8)

For Christ did not send me to baptize, but to preach the gospel—not with words of human wisdom, lest the cross of Christ be emptied of its power.
(1 Corinthians 1:17)

This is what we speak, not in words taught us by human wisdom but in words taught by the Spirit, expressing spiritual truths in spiritual words.
(1 Corinthians 2:13)

78

Deny your personal worries so you can feel distressed for Jesus.

If we are distressed, it is for your comfort and salvation; if we are comforted, it is for your comfort, which produces in you patient endurance of the same sufferings we suffer.
(2 Corinthians 1:6)

The Lord answered her, "Martha, Martha!
You worry and fuss about a lot of things.
There's only one thing you need.
Mary has made the right choice,
and that one thing will not be
taken away from her."
(Luke 10:41–42 GWT)

79

Deny your timetable, plans and works so that you can finish His work.

Tell Archippus: "See to it that you complete the work you have received in the Lord." (Colossians 4:17)

Jesus said to them, "If God were your Father, you would love me, for I came from God and now am here. I have not come on my own; but he sent me. (John 8:42)

I have brought you glory on earth by completing the work you gave me to do. (John 17:4)

Therefore Jesus told them, "The right time for me has not yet come; for you any time is right. (John 7:6)

80

Deny your obligations so you can please the Father.

Still another said, "I will follow you, Lord; but first let me go back and say good-by to my family." Jesus replied, "No one who puts his hand to the plow and looks back is fit for service in the kingdom of God."
(Luke 9:61–62)

Elisha then left his oxen and ran after Elijah. "Let me kiss my father and mother good-by," he said, "and then I will come with you." "Go back," Elijah replied.
"What have I done to you?"
So Elisha left him and went back.
He took his yoke of oxen and slaughtered them. He burned the plowing equipment to cook the meat and gave it to the people, and they ate. Then he set out to follow Elijah and became his attendant.
(1 Kings 19:20–21)

81

Deny your holidays so you can celebrate holy days.

They worshiped the Lord, but they also served their own gods in accordance with the customs of the nations from which they had been brought.
(2 Kings 17:33)

You must not worship the Lord your God in their way.
(Deuteronomy 12:4)

"Therefore come out from them and be separate, says the Lord. Touch no unclean thing, and I will receive you." "I will be a Father to you, and you will be my sons and daughters, says the Lord Almighty."
(2 Corinthians 6:17–18)

Since we have these promises, dear friends, let us purify ourselves from everything that contaminates body and spirit, perfecting holiness out of reverence for God.
(2 Corinthians 7:1)

. . . for it is written:
"Be holy, because I am holy."
(1 Peter 1:16)

82

Deny your religious traditions so that you do not nullify the word of God.

Thus you nullify the word of God by your tradition that you have handed down. And you do many things like that.
(Mark 7:13)

"Woe to you Pharisees, . . .
(Luke 11:42)

83

Deny your father's funeral so you can become free to do God's will.

Another disciple said to him,
"Lord, first let me go and bury my father."
But Jesus told him, "Follow me, and let
the dead bury their own dead."
(Matthew 8:21–22)

Jesus loved Martha and her sister and
Lazarus. Yet when he heard that Lazarus
was sick, he stayed where he was
two more days.
(John 11:5-6)

"Anyone who loves his father or mother
more than me is not worthy of me;
anyone who loves his son or daughter
more than me is not worthy of me;
(Matthew 10:37)

84

Deny your quiet times so you can wrestle in prayer.

Epaphras, who is one of you and a servant of Christ Jesus, sends greetings. He is always wrestling in prayer for you, that you may stand firm in all the will of God, mature and fully assured.
(Colossians 4:12)

During the days of Jesus' life on earth, he offered up prayers and petitions with loud cries and tears to the one who could save him from death, and he was heard because of his reverent submission.
(Hebrews 5:7)

85

Deny your confidence so you can trust in God.

You were wearied by all your ways, but you would not say, 'It is hopeless.' You found renewal of your strength, and so you did not faint.
(Isaiah 57:10)

But the righteousness that is by faith says: "Do not say in your heart, 'Who will ascend into heaven?'" (that is, to bring Christ down) "or 'Who will descend into the deep?'" (that is, to bring Christ up from the dead).
(Romans 10:6–7)

So God will choose the one to whom he decides to show mercy; his choice does not depend on what people want or try to do.
(Romans 9:16 NCV)

86

Deny your money so you can hate and despise it.

"No servant can serve two masters. Either he will hate the one and love the other, or he will be devoted to the one and despise the other. You cannot serve both God and Money." The Pharisees, who loved money, heard all this and were sneering at Jesus.
(Luke 16:13–14)

So if you have not been trustworthy in handling worldly wealth, who will trust you with true riches?
(Luke 16:11)

The brother in humble circumstances ought to take pride in his high position.
(James 1:9)

87

Deny your savings so you can have treasures in heaven.

But store up for yourselves treasures in heaven, where moth and rust do not destroy, and where thieves do not break in and steal.
(Matthew 6:20)

When Jesus heard this, he said to him, "You still lack one thing.
Sell everything you have and give to the poor, and you will have treasure in heaven.
Then come, follow me."
(Luke 18:22)

88

Deny what you read so you can think on good things.

Finally, brothers, whatever is true, whatever is noble, whatever is right, whatever is pure, whatever is lovely, whatever is admirable—if anything is excellent or praiseworthy—think about such things.
(Philippians 4:8)

Words from wise people are like sharp sticks used to guide animals. They are like nails that have been driven in firmly. Altogether they are wise teachings that come from one Shepherd. So be careful, my son, about other teachings. People are always writing books, and too much study will make you tired.
(Ecclesiastes 12:11–12 NCV)

I will set before my eyes no vile thing.
(Psalm 101:3)

89

Deny your thoughts so you can have the thoughts of Jesus.

"For who has known the mind of the
Lord that he may instruct him?"
But we have the mind of Christ.
(1 Corinthians 2:16)

The Lord knows the thoughts of man;
he knows that they are futile.
(Psalm 94:11)

90

Deny what you choose to watch so you can see only what is clean.

The eye is the lamp of the body. If your eyes are good, your whole body will be full of light. But if your eyes are bad, your whole body will be full of darkness. If then the light within you is darkness, how great is that darkness!
(Matthew 6:22–23)

91

Deny your gloom so you can give thanks in all circumstances.

. . . give thanks in all circumstances,
for this is God's will for you
in Christ Jesus.
(1 Thessalonians 5:18)

Rejoice in the Lord always.
I will say it again:
Rejoice!
(Philippians 4:4)

92

Deny your discouragement so you can win with God.

He will not falter or be discouraged till he
establishes justice on earth.
In his law the islands will put their hope.
(Isaiah 42:4)

You sympathized with those
in prison and joyfully accepted the
confiscation of your property,
because you knew that you yourselves
had better and lasting possessions.
So do not throw away your confidence;
it will be richly rewarded.
(Hebrews 10:34–35)[86]

93

Deny your grumbling so you can obey the Lord.

They grumbled in their tents and
did not obey the Lord.
(Psalm 106:25)

And do not grumble, as some of them did—
and were killed by the destroying angel.
(1 Corinthians 10:10)

94

Deny your will, so that you can joyfully do everything others ask you to do—without complaint.

Do *everything* without complaining or arguing, so that you may become blameless and pure, children of God without fault in a crooked and depraved generation, in which you shine like stars in the universe as you hold out the word of life—in order that I may boast on the day of Christ that I did not run or labor for nothing. (Philippians 2:14–16)

95

Deny that God will do special things through you so you can become a humble servant.

You save the humble, but your eyes are on the haughty to bring them low.
(2 Samuel 22:28)

. . . and whoever wants to be first must be slave of all.
(Mark 10:44)

Who, being in very nature God, did not consider equality with God something to be grasped,
(Philippians 2:6)

. . . but made himself nothing, taking the very nature of a servant, being made in human likeness.
(Philippians 2:7)

96

Deny favors done for you so they can be poured out to God.

David longed for water and said, "Oh, that someone would get me a drink of water from the well near the gate of Bethlehem!" So the three mighty men broke through the Philistine lines, drew water from the well near the gate of Bethlehem and carried it back to David. But he refused to drink it; instead, he poured it out before the Lord. (2 Samuel 23:15–16)

97

Deny your Christian music so you can discern what is holy.

Her priests do violence to my law and profane my holy things; they do not distinguish between the holy and the common; they teach that there is no difference between the unclean and the clean; and they shut their eyes to the keeping of my Sabbaths, so that I am profaned among them. (Ezekiel 22:26)

My eyes will be on the faithful in the land, that they may dwell with me; he whose walk is blameless will minister to me. No one who practices deceit will dwell in my house; no one who speaks falsely will stand in my presence. (Psalm 101:6–7)

When Aaron saw this, he built an altar in front of the calf and announced, "Tomorrow there will be a festival to the Lord." . . . Then the Lord said to Moses, "Go down, because your people, whom you brought up out of Egypt, have become corrupt. (Exodus 32:5–7)

98

Deny your salvation so that others can be saved.

For I could wish that I myself were cursed
and cut off from Christ
for the sake of my brothers,
those of my own race,
(Romans 9:3)

99

Deny your interests so you can mature in Jesus.

The seed that fell among thorns stands for those who hear, but as they go on their way they are choked by life's worries, riches and pleasures, and they do not mature.
(Luke 8:14)

Since everything will be destroyed in this way, what kind of people ought you to be?
(2 Peter 3:11)

100

Deny your pride, women, so that you can wear a sign of authority.[87]

For this reason, and because of the angels, the woman ought to have a sign of authority on her head. (1 Corinthians 11:10)

101

Deny your denial of self so you can follow the Spirit.

Such regulations indeed have an appearance of wisdom, with their self-imposed worship, their false humility and their harsh treatment of the body, but they lack any value in restraining sensual indulgence. (Colossians 2:23)

Chapter 11

Led of the Spirit

It is a good exercise for over-enthusiastic people to give up their own ways of practicing self-denial, and to allow God to bring whatever he will into their lives. If you are not willing to accept the self-denials appointed by God, then don't trust the self-denials that you come up with.

—Francois Fenelon

11

I tell you the truth, when you were younger you dressed yourself and went where you wanted; but when you are old you will stretch out your hands, and someone else will dress you and lead you where you do not want to go." Jesus said this to indicate the kind of death by which Peter would glorify God. Then he said to him, "Follow me!" Peter turned and saw that the disciple whom Jesus loved was following them. (This was the one who had leaned back against Jesus at the supper and had said, "Lord, who is going to betray you?") When Peter saw him, he asked, "Lord, what about him?" Jesus answered, "If I want him to remain alive until I return, what is that to you? You must follow me." (John 21:18–22)

"What about him?" Peter asked. Jesus had just told Peter how he would glorify God upon his death and all Peter could wonder about was how John would die. Jesus solidly rebuked Peter saying . . . "What is that to you? You must follow me." God applies the denying of self in different ways and measures in each person's life.[88] While the requirement to deny self unto death is for all, the manner and amount is as varied as God's creation. Our concern should not be what we think God demands of others, but what the Holy Spirit requires of us. It took Peter many years for God to get through to him on this lesson. Like Peter, we always think our cross is harder and that someone else should deny themselves in the same way and manner as we do. We must deny our thoughts that judge others apart from the expressed impression of the Holy Spirit. Testing that to make sure we are first dead to ourselves.

When it comes to helping someone discover how they should deny themselves, this attitude must first become a solid reality by the Holy Spirit. It is none of our business how another does or does not deny himself, unless the Holy Spirit makes it our business. Jesus is the Good Shepherd and it is only as we are "led" of the Spirit to deal with the self unto obedience, do we find the new life. Only Jesus knows what is best for each person and you must serve Him alone.[89] Deny yourself in all that He calls you to and instruct no man of what is required of him unless you have heard from the Holy Spirit to do so.[90]

As the Scripture below instructs us, our denying of self will only produce fruit if it is "by the Spirit."

> For if you live according to the sinful nature, you will die; but if by the Spirit you put to death the misdeeds of the body, you will live, because those who are led by the Spirit of God are sons of God. (Romans 8:13–14)

Not only must we be "led by the Spirit" to be "sons of God" but we must also put to "death the misdeeds of the body," by the power of the Holy Spirit. Just following the Bible never saves a man. As Jesus pointed out, many "diligently study the Scriptures because" they "think that by them" they "posses eternal life," yet refuse to come to Jesus in order that all of their Bible study becomes real. The cross is too painful and costly and they would rather just study the issue than actually deny self.

> You diligently study the Scriptures because you think that by them you possess eternal life. These are the Scriptures that testify about me, yet you refuse to come to me to have life. (John 5:39–40)

Become Losers

Most have not really heard God's voice because they have not done the first two parts of what Jesus demanded. They have not denied themselves and then picked up a cross.[91] There is no way to follow Jesus or to hear His voice unless we have become losers who hate our own lives.[92]

As Romans tell us, only as we "offer our bodies as living sacrifices," which requires much denying of self, will we be in a position to be transformed. Those who seek to by-pass this follow their own emotions, imaginations, and thoughts. It is only after this denial of self has begun that a person is then "able to test and approve what God's will is." So many falsely believe they are doing God's will, but never pass their thoughts through the denying of self and the cross. Such individuals fully deceive themselves into thinking they are doing God's will, when it is themselves they serve.

> Therefore, I urge you, brothers, in view of God's mercy, to offer your bodies as living sacrifices, holy and pleasing to God—this is your spiritual act of worship. Do not conform any longer to the pattern of this world, but be transformed by the renewing of your mind. Then you will be able to test and approve what God's will is—his good, pleasing and perfect will. (Romans 12:1-2)

In other words, follow the Holy Spirit to your death and the Word will be made alive in and through you. Walking to that death will require much denial of self. Doing anything less is to become a legalistic Pharisee or a wide road Christian who will not enter through heaven's gates.

To always be led of the Spirit means that at all times we never are allowed to do what we want.[93] Let us not approach these 101 ways to deny self with a stubborn heart. Rather, with excitement and a growing love for Jesus, let us rejoice in the grace that calls and enables us to deny self. Let us especially ensure that all of self is denied in our ministry work. Rich blessings await those who do so.[94]

Therefore since all power, grace, mercy, and love are available, let us begin to "aim for perfection" when it comes to denying self. With Paul I say "good-bye" to you as you finish this book and admonish you with all joy to "aim for perfection." I encourage you to follow Jesus, denying self, and the "God of love and peace will be with you."

> Finally, brothers, good-by. Aim for perfection, listen to my appeal, be of one mind, live in peace. And the God of love and peace will be with you. (2 Corinthians 13:11)

Everything Said

With everything said, I point you to Jesus and the offensive cross that will make all of this and more a reality.

> I want to know Christ and the power of his resurrection and the fellowship of sharing in his sufferings, becoming like him in his death, and so, somehow, to attain to the resurrection from the dead. (Philippians 3:10–11)

Acknowledgment of Quotes

Bohn, H.G. *The Promises of God* (Bloomington, MN: Garborg's Heart 'n Home, copyright 1988).

Chambers, Oswald. *My Utmost for His Highest* (Grand Rapids, MI: Discovery House, copyright 1992).

Fenelon, Francois. *The Seeking Heart* (Sargent, GA: The Seed Sowers, copyright 1992).

Kirkwood, David S. *The Great Gospel Deception* (Pittsburgh, PA: Ethos Press, copyright 1999). Page 109

Molinos, Michael. *The Spiritual Guide* (Sargent, GA: Seedsowers, copyright 1982). Page 73

Schlink, Basilea. *You Will Never Be the Same* (Minneapolis, MN: Fellowship Bethany, copyright 1972). Page 166

Small, Dwight Hervey. *No Rival Love* (Fort Washington, PA: Christian Literature Crusade, Inc., copyright 1983). Page 85

Tozer, A.W. *Man: The Dwelling Place of God* (Camp Hill, PA: Christian Publications, copyright 1966). Page 73

Watson, Thomas. *Heaven Taken by Storm* (Morgan, PA: Soli Deo Gloria, copyright 1994). Page 63

Wesley, John. *Books for the Ages Version 2.0* (Albany, OR: Ages Software, copyright 1996–1997). Page 87

Endnotes

1. Acts 3:26, *Insanity in the Church* by Timothy Williams. ISBN 1-57921-390-1
2. 1 Peter 2:2
3. Mark 8:35
4. Matthew 5:3–4
5. 1 Peter 2:2, Hebrews 6:1
6. Matthew 7:21
7. 1 Corinthians 8:2
8. Matthew 3:11
9. Matthew 7:21
10. 2 Timothy 4:7, Galatians 6:17
11. 1 Peter 4:1
12. Matthew 5:20, Matthew 28:20, Hebrews 5:8–9, Hebrews 12:14, 1 John 2:4
13. Philippians 2:12–13
14. Luke 6:46
15. Galatians 3:3
16. Exodus 32:5, notice whose name the golden calf was built in.

17. Luke 20:35
18. Matthew 3:15, *Even The Demons Believe* by Timothy Williams explains this in greater detail. ISBN 1-57921-355-3
19. John 4:24
20. Romans 10:5, Galatians 3:12, Romans 10:5–7
21. Hosea 12:6, Hebrews 4:11
22. *The Essential Piece* by Timothy Williams. ISBN 1-57921-293-x
23. John 19:23–24
24. Acts 2:38
25. (1 Peter 3:21) and this water symbolizes baptism that *now saves you* also—not the removal of dirt from the body but the pledge of a good conscience toward God. It *saves you by the resurrection* of Jesus Christ,
26. (John 6:65) He went on to say, "This is why I told you that no one can come to me unless the Father *has enabled* him."
27. 1 Corinthians 1:17, *Even the Demons Believe* by Timothy Williams explains this in greater detail. ISBN 1-57921-355-3
28. Psalm 84:7
29. Galatians 6:8
30. Romans 10:10, 2 Corinthians 2:15, 1 Peter 1:5, 1 Corinthians 1:18, Ephesians 2:5, Philippians 1:28, 2 Timothy 1:9, Hebrews 9:28, 1 Thessalonians 5:8, Romans 8:24, Ephesians 1:13–14, Romans 13:11, Ephesians 1:4–5
31. Job 4:18, Revelation 22:2 Though we will not sin in heaven, God alone is the only one who is perfect, or as Jesus put it, is the only one who is "good." See Mark 10:18

32. Luke 8:13; note they are believers, for they "believe" but only for "a while." But as testing comes, they "fall away." (Luke 8:13) Those on the rock are the ones who receive the word with joy when they hear it, but they have no root. They believe for a while, but in the time of testing they fall away.
33. Galatians 5:4
34. Hebrews 6:4–6
35. 2 Corinthians 11:4
36. John 15:5
37. 2 Corinthians 10:18
38. Hebrews 10:29
39. Mark 2:9
40. Acts 3:26, Acts 11:18, 2 Timothy 2:25
41. Romans 3:11
42. Hebrews 11:3, Acts 16:14
43. 1 Corinthians 15:1, Romans 4:9, James 2:21–22
44. Jude :24, Romans 11:22
45. 2 Timothy 4:10, 1 Timothy 1:18–19, Hebrews 6:4–8, Galatians 6:9
46. 1 Corinthians 15:10
47. James 2:18
48. 2 Corinthians 13:5
49. 1 Peter 1:2, Hebrews 9:14
50. Hebrews 3:12, Romans 5:17, Ephesians 3:7
51. Luke 9:23
52. Romans 3:10–18, Genesis 6:6, Colossians 3:5–6, Psalms 51:3–5
53. Jude :14–15
54. 1 John 2:15, 2 Peter 3:11, 1 Peter 4:4, Luke 17:32
55. Luke 14:32
56. Luke 9:23
57. Galatians 2:20

58. John 6:26
59. Titus 2:14
60. Hebrews 6:7–9
61. Psalm 17:14
62. Ephesians 4:31
63. Matthew 11:17, Luke 7:32
64. Matthew 5:22
65. James 5:16
66. 2 Corinthians 7:10–11, 2 Timothy 2:19, Acts 20:21
67. Luke 6:48
68. 1 Peter 4:18
69. At the writing of this book, I am 45 years old.
70. 2 Timothy 2:22
71. Mark 9:43–45
72. Proverbs 22:14
73. 1 Corinthians 10:12
74. Only as we "hate" our concepts and ways of showing love, will God's true pure love flow into our lives. For a detailed look at this obtain a copy of *The Essential Piece* by Timothy Williams
75. Genesis 3:11
76. *A Whisper Revival, Our Only Option* By Timothy Williams. ISBN 1-57921-274-3
77. Commentaries are fine in the Lord, provided the Holy Spirit directs. Only as we are dead to our intellectual perusing of Bible knowledge can the Holy Spirit direct and illuminate.
78. It is not without irony that today everyone seems to want to know what the Greek says. Like the Greeks, we are more impressed with wisdom than with being taught by the Holy Spirit.
79. Call to get your free sermon "Let Your Lifeboat Go" (360) 802-2550

80. Jesus had no reason to weep. He knew Lazarus would shortly be resurrected. He could have chosen not to burden Himself with weeping. He who had no reason to weep, wept because others wept.
81. The same wisdom, love, and care that God used to make the soul and the spirit He used to create our bodies. God gave the same amount of attention to our bodies as He did to our hearts. It is not true that God only looks to the heart. Indeed, how we dress and behave is a reflection of our hearts. Therefore Scripture tells us to glorify God whether by word or deed. A quick glance at the Old Testament makes clear that God desires we dress in accordance with His glory and will.
82. The only way our names are written in heaven is if we obey Jesus.
83. The seraphs covered their eyes so they could not see their beauty. They covered their feet so that they could not see their works.
84. One becomes enlightened by Scripture only by presenting oneself to God to be crucified. To be presentable to God we must have the Bible in our hands and a cross on our back. Merely to study the Bible with all our human effort makes us contemptible Pharisees. We must deny our Bible Study so that we do not preach "ink" (2 Cor. 3:3).
85. A person may hold a public office so long as he is crucified to that office.
86. This is a not a prosperity confidence, but a cross confidence. A confidence that is true faith and arises even when we feel totally helpless and weak. When our situation is not prosperous for the flesh, but is

being tormented by the cross, we still trust God. That is true faith.

87. Call and request the free sermon "Sign of Authority" (360) 802-2550
88. Luke 2:25 compared to 2:36–37.
89. Matthew 20:1–16
90. Colossians 1:28–29
91. Romans 12:1–2
92. Mark 8:35, John 12:25, Romans 12:1–2, 1 Peter 4:2
93. Galatians 5:17
94. Acts 3:26